THE TRUTH ABOUT FAIRIES

Elves, Gnomes, Goblins & the Little People

Philip Ardagh writes both fiction and
non-fiction, and is a familiar face at book festivals
in England, Scotland and Wales. His books have
been translated into numerous languages,
including Latin.

THE TRUTH ABOUT FAIRIES

Elves, Gnomes, Goblins
& the Little People

Philip Ardagh

Illustrated by Jason Cox

MACMILLAN CHILDREN'S BOOKS

First published 2005 by Macmillan Children's Books
a division of Macmillan Publishers Ltd
20 New Wharf Road, London N1 9RR
Basingstoke and Oxford
www.panmacmillan.com

Associated companies throughout the world

ISBN 1 405 04750 X

1 3 5 7 9 8 6 4 2

A CIP ctalogue record for this book is available from the British Library.

Printed in China

Up the airy mountain,
Down the rushy glen,
We daren't go a-hunting,
For fear of little men.

From *The Fairies*
– William Allingham (1824–89)

Contents

Changelings

Once in a while, bad or mischievous fairies (and dwarfs) are known to steal a human baby and to swap it with one of their own. This impostor child is known as a changeling – having been changed with the real thing – and could be anything from a fairy to an elf or a gnome, or even a lump of carved wood magically brought to life. Something that all changelings have in common though is that, to the human eye, they look very ugly indeed, and often seem stupid or lazy.

1

The secret of laughter

It's one thing for parents to be suspicious that a changeling isn't really their own child and another thing to prove it. There's also the problem of getting your own baby back. In many parts of the world, the secret lies with laughter, and just about the only way to make changelings laugh is to show them something they've never seen before. (This is because, according to some theories, despite taking the place of a child, they are, in truth, incredibly old and therefore think that the world has nothing new to show them.)

Eggshells

A common story of how a mother tricked a changeling is told in different versions across the world, from Ireland to Japan, and involves eggshells. One telling of this tale has the mother using an eggshell as a saucepan to boil water. Another has her staggering around with a beer-filled eggshell as though it is incredibly heavy. In each instance the changeling, who's been watching from his bed, can't believe his eyes and bursts out laughing. Moments later, he's disappeared, and the mother's true baby has – more often than not – been returned.

Up, up and away

Some mothers have risked more drastic action. This has included holding the changeling above a red-hot coal shovel then letting go of him . . . Rather than risk burning, the changeling flies up the chimney – or through the roof – to escape, and the real baby usually comes home safe and sound. This isn't recommended though, in case the child turns out not to be a changeling after all!

Deep in the hillside

In a story from the Western Isles of Scotland, a blacksmith managed to prove his so-called son was

3

a changeling and chased him off, but had to find a way to get his own son back. He discovered that the boy was being held by the little people inside a small round hill (variously called the Green Knoll or the Green Knowe). Here they forged metal weapons in a mighty furnace. As the son of a blacksmith, they thought the boy could help them in this task. (The reason for stealing human babies was often to put them to work.)

At night, when a magic door opened in the knoll – which would close again at the first light of dawn – the blacksmith sneaked inside. Using his Bible to protect himself from fairy magic, he also slipped a cockerel out from under his coat. Seeing the light of the forge's furnace, the cock crowed, thinking it was daybreak. The little people panicked, believing dawn had come and that the magic door would close, leaving some of their mischief-making number trapped outside. The blacksmith grabbed his son with one hand and,

4

still holding the Bible in his other, they made good their escape.

Another possibility

There are, of course, those who argue that there are no such things as changelings. It's human nature to say that a lazy, ugly or 'stupid' child is not really their own and must have been swapped at birth! As for the grass hummocks, these are often prehistoric burial chambers or 'barrows'.

Fairy Rings

Look carefully and you'll sometimes see dark green circles in the grass of a field or a meadow or even a lawn. Sometimes they are even surrounded by a ring of mushrooms. Some people will tell you that this is the spot where a mare has given birth to a baby foal. The general consensus, however, is that this is a fairy ring: a magical circle in which fairies meet to dance. It's best to leave them well alone. Fairies don't take kindly to people interfering with such rings. Those foolish enough not to heed such warnings have been said to go lame, blind or even get carried off by the fairies.

Carolling

In medieval times, dancing in a circle – carolling – was a common practice, even in church around the pillars. As time went by, fashions changed and carolling was dropped. Dancing in a circle was seen as old-fashioned, then un-Christian or even sinister. It became associated with witches and fairies. And where better for fairies to be assumed to dance than in these mysterious rings?

Fungi to dance with

And the fairy rings themselves? Scientists will tell you that these are caused by a particular fungus (*Marasmius oreades*, if you must know) and the reason why they survive is that grazing animals steer clear of them. They don't taste nice.

*Your demi-puppets that
By moonshine do the green sour ringlets make,
Whereof the ewe not bites.*

From *The Tempest*
– William Shakespeare (1564–1616)

ℱairy Tales

The problem with calling fairy tales 'fairy tales' is that they very rarely have fairies in them. (This misleading name probably dates back to an English translation of a book by Madame d'Aulnoy, called *Les Contes des Fees*, published in France in 1697.)

The problem with people's genuine beliefs about fairies – their local fairy folklore, if you like – is that most have been lost, because they were part of an oral tradition: they were spoken and rarely written down. This means that we're in left in the rather strange position of having lots of made-up fairy tales (which no one really believed) and far fewer genuine fairy folk tales.

Well-known names

Probably the most famous collectors and retellers of fairy tales were the German brothers Jakob and Wilhelm Grimm, better known as the Brothers Grimm. Their fairy tales were first published from 1812–14. Many of their versions of these now-familiar classics were very gruesome indeed. Another famous writer of fairy tales was the Danish son of a shoemaker, Hans Christian Andersen.

The British Isles

Although surviving English fairy tales are generally of the light-hearted *Jack-and-the-Beanstalk* variety, many more Scottish, Welsh and Irish tales of true fairy folklore have survived as part of the Celtic tradition.

In Scotland, there are tales of 'fairy fights' on Halloween and of fairy mice riding the backs of livestock, paralysing the poor animals. In Wales, there are tales of the Tylwyth Teg, a race of small beings, no bigger than seven-year-olds, living on the isle of Anglesey. And as for Ireland, it's one of the richest sources of fairy folklore in the world.

Every man's life is a fairy tale
written by God's finger.

From *Preface to Works*
– Hans Christian Andersen (1805–75)

Fairy Godmothers

The one notable exception to the you'll-very-rarely-find-fairies-in-fairy-tales rule is fairy godmothers. It was a fairy godmother who put Sleeping Beauty to sleep (rather than letting her die), and another fairy godmother who turned the pumpkin and mice into Cinderella's coach and horses.

But what is a fairy godmother? As the name implies, she's always a female fairy and seems to be of the motherly-with-wings variety. She also seems to be the type that can use those wings effectively to fly (see pages 26 to 28), and is good at magic in general and in granting wishes in particular. People often talk of a 'guardian angel' looking out for them, and a fairy godmother seems to fill a similar role.

Tom Thumb

A well-known, but slightly less popular, fairy tale than *Sleeping Beauty* and *Cinderella* is *Tom Thumb*. The first two fairy tales came to England from France in the eighteenth century, but Tom Thumb and his fairy godmother had been around since the 1620s. (In the tale she tries to protect the tiny hero from the dangers of the big wide world.)

Animal friends

Funnily enough, earlier traditional versions of *Sleeping Beauty* and *Cinderella* apparently had magical animals rather than fairy godmothers helping the heroine. Nowadays, of course, fairy godmothers regularly appear in books, pantomimes and plays, and on TV and in films.

I think, at a child's birth, if a mother could ask a fairy godmother to endow it with the most useful gift, that gift would be curiosity.

– Eleanor Roosevelt (1884–1962)

Fairy Wind

The fairy wind is best known in Irish folklore, where it's called *seidean si*. Fairy wind can be anything from a sudden gust to a whirlwind, and can be caused by a whole variety of different fairy activity. Sometimes the fairies are thought to be caught up in the wind as they ride across the skies. On other occasions, it's said to be caused by a passing fairy (in much the same way that a passing car causes a slipstream of air).

The good, the bad and the frightening

A simple eddy of fairy wind in a hayfield is said to be an omen of good weather for making hay because it's a sign that the fairies are lending a helping hand. If the sky turns dark when there's a gust of fairy wind, though, more likely than not it means that a soul is departing this world.

Worst of all, a bad fairy wind is known to harm livestock and humans, sometimes indiscriminately, but sometimes specific people who fear that the fairies are 'coming for them'.

Off with the roof

Fairies are generally set in their ways and don't like it when a human's change in habits inconveniences them. If, say, a man starts using a door in a house that's been closed for many years, a sudden blast of fairy wind may whip the whole roof off.

Protecting their property

The people who need to be most wary of the fairy wind are those intent on stealing fairy treasure. Sometimes it's just a warning but, if the thief doesn't heed it, far nastier things might happen.

And it's not just treasure. Legend has it that a musician once stole some fairy tunes and was audacious – and silly – enough to play them at a local dance. No sooner had he played the first few notes than he was plucked from the ground by a blast of wind, never to be seen again.

Human nature

It's human nature to try to make sense of natural occurrences – winds, floods, volcanic eruptions and the like   and you can see why fairies might get the blame. By the same token, opening a window or a door in a house can create a sudden through-draught, causing other doors to slam or objects to fall . . . all of which can, once again, be blamed on the little people. As for fairy winds being omens of the weather, folklore is full of different kinds of weather forecasting, from the red sky at night to sitting-down cows!

Any man can lose his hat in a fairy wind.

– Irish proverb

Fairy Food

Before I go any further, if you're ever offered food by a fairy, DON'T EAT IT. There are a whole host of tales about children about to eat the most delicious 'dainties' offered them by a mysterious woman. Fortunately for them, they're saved in the nick of time before the merest morsel has passed their lips. Fortunately because if you eat fairy food you're unlikely to be able to return to 'the land of men'. In other words, you're enchanted and not in a good way.

Mouse soup

There are notable exceptions, though, the most famous of which must be mouse soup. It's believed that, in Ireland in particular, one spoonful from a fairy's bowl of mouse soup is enough to give one the Sight: the ability to see fairies (see pages 24 to 25).

A pinch of salt

Fairies are said to have a similar diet to humans but with one important difference. They can't abide salt. (It can destroy magic.) Fairies aren't too fussy about how they lay their hands on food either. They'll beg, borrow or steal. If a fairy (in the guise of a human) borrows butter, you'd be wise to give it to them. They'll always return the same amount and may even bring you luck. Refuse them and, at best, you'll be on the receiving end of some fairy mischief. At worst, their pranks could even kill you.

How do you know if someone is actually a fairy in disguise? You don't, so it's best to be generous to all strangers.

Milking the farmer dry

Though known to drink everything from whisky to the nectar from flowers, a fairy's favourite drink is milk. In Ireland, there's an age old tradition of letting the first drops of milk from a cow's udder fall to the ground, rather than being put in the pail. This is for the fairies.

There are many reports of fairies actually milking cows in the field. In some cases, it's the cows that have been milked by fairy hands that are never ill. In others, the cows have become diseased or even died. Some farmers used to leave a cow in the herd solely for the fairies' use.

Unwanted milk should be poured on the ground outside for fairies. (It won't attract them to the neighbourhood but, if they're already there, they'll appreciate it.) It's the same with spilt milk. It's rightfully theirs.

Sharing the joy

In parts of Brittany (which shares many Celtic traditions) there's an old custom of leaving food out for the fairies at a child's birth. It's believed that fairies attend all human births and – particularly with the fear of changelings – it makes sense to keep on the right side of them, perhaps even bringing the newborn child a happy, charmed life. A table of salt-free food is laid in the actual room where the babe will be born.

A salty issue

Salt used to be a very valuable commodity. The word 'salary' comes from the Latin word for salt because Roman soldiers used to be paid with it. It's also a preservative. Not putting salt on food supposedly left out for fairies could have come about for these reasons rather than magical ones. It was too valuable to waste, and the food would perish – and apparently be 'eaten' – more quickly. Just a thought.

Fairy loaves

Fairy loaves is the name given to fossilized sea urchins because of their appearance. Also known as 'sand dollars', sea urchins are not only the shape of very small circular loaves but even have the criss-cross pattern at the top that is common on cottage loaves.

To See or Not To See?

One possible reason for not being able to see fairies could be that they don't exist. Discounting this, for the sake of argument, leaves three distinct possibilities as to why you may never have seen one: firstly, they go to great lengths not to be seen; secondly, you've never actually been anywhere where fairies live or, thirdly, they're invisible.

Some people believe that there are no fairies on mainland Britain any more because they fled the island when the Puritans came to power in the seventeenth century. The Puritans banned many fun things, including dancing and celebrating Christmas, so the fairies are thought to have had enough and left for happier climes. (Not everyone is convinced by this, believing that at least some stayed behind.)

In places where there are still said to be fairies, however, the invisibility argument is strong. Why? Because people with the Sight, or who use special spells, potions or ointment (see page 30), can often see fairies when the rest of us can't.

> *There never was a merry world since the fairies left off dancing . . .*
>
> From *Table Talk*
> – John Selden (1584–1654)

To Fly or Not To Fly?

It may come as a surprise, but even those varieties of fairies with wings are not necessarily said to fly well unaided. Fairies can hover off the ground or flutter from flower to flower, but often prefer to fly on a twig or on the stem of a flower (usually ragwort) in much the same way that a witch – or Harry Potter, for that matter – is said to ride a broomstick.

If a whole swarm of fairies (sometimes referred to as a troop) go out riding in the sky together, they can cause the fairy winds described on pages 15 to 18.

26

A traditional fairy cry to activate their stems into flying mode – and to keep them up there – is 'Horse and hattock!' (a hattock being nothing more than a small hat).

Landing in hot water

One tale has it that a Scottish laird was out in his fields one day when he saw a huge cloud of dust above him and heard the 'Horse and hattock!' cry. Somewhat puzzled, he repeated the words, only to find himself being whisked away.

They all came to land in the cellar of the palace of the King of France, where the fairies handed the laird a cup and together they sampled the royal wines. After a heavy night's drinking, the laird awoke to find himself with a thumping headache and in deep trouble.

Though puzzled how the Scotsman had got into his cellar, the king thought him a thief and didn't believe his story . . . until, that is, the laird showed

27

him the fairy cup. It was of such beauty and delicate craftsmanship that the King of France was convinced that it could only have been made by fairy hands. He let the laird go, who returned to his home in Duffus, east of Inverness, where the gold cup took pride of place among his family's most treasured possessions.

The Fairy Realm

Although fairies seem to spend a fair amount of time in the world of us mortals, causing mischief and sometimes mayhem, tales tell of a world of their own: fairyland.

Fairyland is ruled over by a king and queen (see page 34), but it would appear that the king generally leaves it up to the queen to make most of the important decisions. Here, the fairies live in houses, attend feasts and spend a great deal of time eating, drinking and making merry. Much is made from gold and silver, and everyone is beautiful and lives forever. Despite this lack of death, new fairies are born all the time (often looked after by kidnapped human midwives).

With this ever-increasing population, it's statistically likely that fairyland is either very large, very heavily populated, or both.

With eyes to see

Apparently, human 'visitors' to fairyland have to have their eyes rubbed with a magical fairy ointment in order to be able to see the fairies. Those who are released (or, more likely, escape) without having the ointment removed are then able to see fairies whenever they put in an appearance.

Fairy pets

There aren't only fairies – and the occasional stolen mortal – in fairyland. There are also two domesticated animals: horses and dogs (but no cats, which are strongly associated with witches). Fairy horses are always white and, more often than not, their manes are braided with silver bells that tinkle when they're ridden.

Fairies enjoy pageantry and often parade on their horses, their dogs running alongside them. (But these horses have a far less pleasant side to them, as you'll see on pages 58 to 59.)

Not home to all

Not all types of fairy live in fairyland, however – only those referred to as being members of the fairy nation (or sometimes the fairy race) live there. Other fairies never stray from our world. These are a very different kind of being.

Fairy Time

One thing which many reports from people who claimed to have been in fairyland have in common is the different speed at which time passes. Some claim that time as we know it does not exist there. A person may spend what seems like years in fairyland, only to find that a matter of weeks, days or even simply hours have passed here among the mortals. In one famous instance, the equivalent of 900 years in fairyland is said to have passed in one earthly night.

A likely story!

Non-believers claim that this is for the sake of a good story. A person need only have 'gone' for a short while to be able to tell a whole raft of made-up adventures that would have taken years to have witnessed or actually been a part of. Also, in a short nap you can have dreams stretching a lifetime.

Lovers to bed; 'tis almost fairy time

From *The Merry Wives of Windsor*
– William Shakespeare (1564–1616)

33

The Fairy King & Queen

I n Shakespeare's *A Midsummer Night's Dream*, the king and queen of the fairies are Oberon and Titania and they've fallen out over a changeling (see pages 1 to 5). The beautiful and elegant Queen Titania shouldn't be confused with Queen Mab, who's also a fairy but of a much smaller variety. She's mentioned in Shakespeare's *Romeo & Juliet*, but also appears in the writings of Ben Jonson (1572–1637), among others. Her skills include blistering faces and causing midwives to fall into ditches!

Household Fairies

There are certain types of fairies associated with particular places who have no connection with fairyland. One of the most familiar of these is the household fairies, who share buildings with the humans living in them. Such fairies go by a number of names including billies and kobolds, but they're most commonly known as brownies. Today, of course, the only Brownies you're likely to run into are junior Girl Guides!

Not a pretty sight

Brownies are very hairy, which is important because they don't wear clothes, and hair is good insulation for keeping them warm. They're either attached to one farm or to one family. This makes a big difference.

Good brownies help around the house and can ensure that a farm and its family thrive. These are the kind of brownies you want to come with you if and when you move.

Bad brownies are a different matter. They not only leave gates open for the livestock to escape, or block chimneys, but they can also make cows' milk dry up and even make butter go rancid. These are the sort of brownies that you hope are attached to the farm and not to your family, so you can move and get away from them!

Breaking the bonds

There is one way to cut the ties with a brownie, either to free one who's served you well over the years by way of a 'thank you', or to get rid of the troublesome variety. This is called 'laying' and is a very straightforward procedure. You simply make the brownie some clothes. All they have to do is to put them on and they're freed from the family or farm.

Pixy-led

In the past, the majority of people had to go everywhere on foot, and travelling was even more dangerous than it is today. People didn't generally carry maps and an unfamiliar route could be fraught with hazards from robbers to boggy marshland if you strayed off the beaten track. Few places were lit, and darkness brought even more potential dangers. Then, on top of all this, there were the fairies whose sole intent was to lead the poor traveller astray. Being tricked by fairies in such a way is called being pixy-led.

38

Some fairies lead people astray for mere mischief and no more. There is no real harm done, just time wasted and a few nerves jangled. Unfortunately, other fairies lead humans astray for motives that can only be described as sinister.

Pranksters

Cornish pixies are generally fairies of the former, friendlier, variety. They cast thick mists to make unwary travellers walk round and round and round in endless circles, but only intend to cause a bit of trouble more than real harm. Then there's Robin Goodfellow, who's also called Puck (the name under which he appears as a character in Shakespeare's *A Midsummer Night's Dream*). He too is a prankster. A joker.

Will-o'-the-wisp

Far less fun is the will-o'-the-wisp, who also goes by the name of jack-o'-lantern (though there are those

39

who argue that he too is Puck). Will-o'-the-wisp haunts boggy marshlands, carrying a flickering light to lure travellers off the path, making them believe it is the light of a house or a lantern and leading them into a watery grave. There are others who claim that he's not a fairy but is actually the soul of a man so evil that he's not only been refused entry to heaven but also to hell.

All hot air!

Will-o'-the-wisp is also the name given to the pale glow you sometimes see over marshland, which has a more scientific name of *ignis fatuus*. It's caused by a mixture of gases created by decomposing organic matter (rotting plants and the like). Some non-believers may say that this is how the myth of the evil pixy came into being.

Curing the pixy-led

To avoid being pixy-led, always whistle when you're out and about. If that doesn't work, turn your jacket or coat inside out. Better still, wear a sturdy pair of boots or shoes with plenty of nails in them and carry some salt in your pocket. Both iron and salt work well against magic. Any combination of these things should help protect you from the fairies when you're on your way. Forewarned is forearmed!

Fairy Trees

Different trees are associated with different kinds of fairy, some good, some bad. Elder trees, for example, are in the domain of good fairies and, in the past, it was thought bad luck to cut an elder's branches without asking the fairies first, or without making some kind of offering.

In Ireland, a single hawthorn or a ring of three can mark the entrance to a fairy hideaway in a hollow hill (see pages 3 to 4). Irish fairies, called shee, as in a screaming banshee (spelled *sidhe* in Gaelic), often live in amazing palaces below ground. To fall asleep beneath a hawthorn would be very unwise indeed.

The creeping weeping willow

Even more spooky are weeping willow trees. There's many a tale of weeping willows, enchanted by bad fairies, freeing themselves from the soil and scuttling along riverbanks, preying on passing humans.

Enchanted apple trees

Unfortunately, once in a while, an apple tree might also be enchanted by fairies. It's unfortunate because apples are a very popular fruit with us humans, but an apple off an enchanted tree counts as fairy food. And, as you can see on pages 19 to 23, eating such food can have very serious consequences indeed. A single bite could lead to seven human years in fairyland.

I see men as trees, walking.

From *The King James Bible*
– St Mark

Leprechauns

Of all the little people, the leprechauns – pronounced lepricorns – of Ireland must be among the most famous, appearing on keyrings, T-shirts, anything and everything! Usually pictured wearing green, with big-buckled shoes, a hat and a cheeky grin on his little face, a leprechaun's preferred profession seems to be that of a shoemaker, and his most popular pastime appears to be burying his crocks (pots) of gold at the ends of rainbows.

If you can catch a leprechaun, he has to reveal the whereabouts of his buried treasure. But once you've caught him, if you take your eye off him for so much as an instant, he'll simply vanish into thin air.

Caught on film

The publicity for the 1959 Disney film *Darby O'Gill and the Little People*, starring none other than Sean Connery, later of James Bond 007 fame, gives thanks to 'King Brian of Knocknasheega and his leprechauns, whose gracious co-operation made this picture possible'. The special effects, many of them achieved through a technique called 'forced perspective', are extraordinary even by today's standards.

The Cluricaun

There's a little fellow sometimes referred to as the cluricaun, or the *clobhair-ceann*, who seems to

45

make a career out of getting himself drunk in other people's cellars. There are those who believe that he's a separate kind of fairy to the leprechaun, and those who claim that he's simply a leprechaun who's taking a break from cobbling and is out on a drinking spree!

It weren't me!

Claiming that there were drink-stealing little people about must have been quite handy for servants accused of helping themselves in their masters' cellars!

The Red Man

Another solitary type of fairy, not part of the fairy nation, is the far darrig (from the Gaelic *fear dearg*), which means the red man. He gets his name from the red cap and coat he wears. He is one of the small, wingless fairies, probably closely related to the leprechaun, and is also found in Ireland.

Instead of busying himself making shoes, however, the red man spends his time thinking up and carrying out practical jokes, some of which are very unpleasant!

The Fairy Mistress

One of the most dangerous fairies to young Irishmen is the leanhaun shee, or fairy mistress. The only way for her to survive is to live off the lives of the men who love her. She picks a man and, if he doesn't fall for her, she becomes his slave. If he loves her, however, she draws on his life force and he wastes away and dies. But even in death he is tied to her.

The fairy mistress is said to have been a great inspiration to many poets who died young. She was their muse but also their destroyer.

There is one way to escape from the fairy mistress's clutches, but it is a cruel one. You must find a man to take your place. For you to survive, you risk destroying another man's life.

To wake the soul by tender strokes of art,
To raise the genius, and to mend the heart;
To make mankind, in conscious virtues bold.
Live o'er each scene, and be what they behold:
For this the Tragic Muse first trod the stage.

From the *Prologue to Addison's Cato*
– Alexander Pope (1688–1744)

Wailing Banshees

The name for a banshee comes from the Gaelic *bean* (pronounced ban), meaning woman, and *sidhe* (pronounced shee), meaning fairy. These banshees have a very particular duty in society. It was – and possibly still is – their role to be attached to one of the old Irish families and, when the time comes, to wail before a family member is about to die. To hear a banshee's cry is an omen of death.

If someone of great importance is about to die, more than one banshee will wail their lament.

There'll be a whole chorus of them, wailing and singing as one.

Headless, headless, everywhere!

Sometimes the wailing banshee is accompanied by another omen of impending death, the coach-a-bower (*coiste-bodhar*). This huge black coach, with a coffin on top, is pulled by headless horses – gulp! – and is driven by a headless phantom called a dullahan.

The funeral cry

Some claim that the funeral cry, or keen, made by peasants was made to mimic the wail of the banshee. Others argue that it was the other way around. The whole idea of the banshee was dreamed up from the sound of the funeral cry!

Merrows & Water Nymphs

Whether or not a merrow is actually a type of fairy is open to debate. They're certainly related to mermaids. The females look like beautiful women, except for their fish-like tails and the scales between their fingers. The males are a very different matter: green teeth and hair, red noses and eyes like pigs . . . which is probably why many merrows fall in love with fishermen rather than with their own kind!

To come ashore, merrows have to change their

52

form to get around, so they shape-shift into horn-less cows.

In their true merrow form, they carry or wear a special red cap that, if stolen, means they'll never be able to swim beneath the waves again.

There are stories of Irishmen and Irishwomen descended from sailors married to magical merrows (one assumes in fishy rather than cow-like form).

Lorelei of the Rhine

Lorelei is probably the most famous of all water nymphs, which are also similar to mermaids in appearance. Her favourite spot was a rock in the River Rhine in Germany. There she would sit, luring men to her with her unearthly beauty and her hypnotic song, their vessels smashing on the rocks hidden just below the surface of the water.

According to legend, the son of a certain Count Palatinate died trying to reach her. The heartbroken count sent four soldiers to capture her, ordering them to plug their ears with wax to block out the sound of her magical singing.

The soldiers tried not to look directly at her as they climbed the rocks, so she tried to distract them by plucking the priceless pearls from her hair and throwing them down at them. When this too failed to stop their climb, she called on her father – the spirit of the River Rhine itself – to save her. He created an enormous wave which carried her off the rock to safety, leaving the four brave soldiers clinging to the rock. Lorelei was never seen again. She could lure no more sailors to their deaths.

Water nymphs are sometimes referred to as nixies.

Fairy Doctors

Fairy doctors are probably not what you think. They're humans, not fairies, you see. It's just that they get their power from fairies because they have a special temperament when they're born. Fairies have been known to love certain human babies so much that they've taken them away (see changelings on pages 1 to 5) and have often kept them in fairyland for seven years. (Seven being a very magical number, hence the great significance of being the seventh son of a seventh son.) When returned to the human, earthly world, many such people have become fairy doctors, sought out by others for their advice and healing.

Sometimes those chosen for such a role are not taken by the fairies, but find themselves preferring their own company, and eventually developing their powers and understanding. (Those who don't become fairy doctors under such circumstances might end up as gifted poets or musicians.)

Remarkable powers

Fairy doctors have cures and counter-charms, and can give advice on suspected changelings, milk-less cows and even on the best places to build or not to build so as not to upset the fairies. They can also call on the help and advice of the troop-ing fairies (see page 26) of the fairy realm when needed.

Many fairy doctors don't eat meat or drink alcohol, living mainly off a diet of bread, fruit and vegetables. They also do much to keep the ancient traditions alive. Fairy doctors used to be a common sight in Ireland. Not so today.

Good luck befriend thee, son; for at thy birth
The faery ladies danced upon the hearth;
The drowsy nurse hath sworn she did them spy
Come tripping to the room where thou didst lie,
And sweetly sing round about thy bed
Strew all their blessings on thy sleeping head!

From *At a Vacation Exercise in the College*
– John Milton (1608–74)

Fairy Horses

Fairy horses, also known as kelpie or phooka, may be a part of the beauty and pageantry of fairyland (see pages 30 to 31) but, when they're among us ordinary folk, they take on a far more sinister role.

Fairy horses have been known to appear to children, always near a lake or river or some body of water. They look small and charming and particularly appealing to children: the ideal little pony.

The more children who want to climb up on to

the fairy horse's back, the longer that back becomes, in order to accommodate them all.

Once there are plenty of children mounted on it, enjoying the ride, the fairy horse then gallops into the water, disappearing beneath the surface. It's no good any of the children trying to jump free. Fairy magic keeps them stuck to the animal's back. The kelpie then eats them.

A word of warning

Children have always enjoyed playing in and around water, and children have always drowned in accidents as a consequence. It's possible, of course, that tales of the kelpie simply grew up as a way of parents warning their children to stay away from rivers and lakes.

Dwarfs

Most dwarfs are about a metre tall, have very long beards, work in mines and are amazing metalworkers. In English, the plural of dwarf is dwarfs. Many people assume that it's dwarves, because that's the way the author J. R. R. Tolkien spelled it in his epic fantasy *The Lord of the Rings*.

Most dwarfs are found in, or originally came from, Germany. Although they spend much of the time living or working underground, they don't mind daylight and do come into contact with humans. They've even been known to steal babies, replacing them with changelings (see pages 1 to 5). Weapons made by dwarfs are believed to hold magical power.

Shape-shifting

According to Norse mythology, some dwarfs could change into animals. Famously, one of the sons of the dwarf King Hreidmar turned himself into an otter to go salmon fishing . . . only to be killed by the god Loki in sport and in error! To compensate the dwarf king, the god gave him a hoard of treasure which later turned out to be cursed. Of Hreidmar's two remaining sons, one murdered him and the other changed the course of human history. (This last one's name was Regin.)

Regin, bringer of knowledge

Fleeing his murderous brother and the world of dwarfs, legend has it that Regin went to live among humans. It is said that it was he who first taught humankind how to fashion metal to make tools and weapons, how to harness a plough to an ox (instead of ploughing by hand) and even how to build a house. It seems we have a lot to thank dwarfs for!

The Seven Dwarfs

Walt Disney's *Snow White and the Seven Dwarfs*, made in 1937, was the first ever full-length animated feature film. Before it was released, it was nicknamed 'Disney's Folly', and many thought it was doomed to fail. In fact, it went on to win Disney a special Oscar.

Gnomes

Gnomes are generally smaller than dwarfs, much uglier (to human eyes, that is) and spend all their time underground (hoarding their treasure) and avoiding humans. The gnome's most amazing ability is to be able to walk through solid earth as easily as a human walks through air or a fish swims through water. This is fortunate, for gnomes can never walk above ground in sunlight. The light from a single sunbeam would be enough to turn a gnome to stone. This is why humans and gnomes rarely meet, though miners are said to sometimes hear the tap-tap-tapping of gnomes deep in their mineshafts. The name gnome comes from the Greek ge-nomos, which simply means earth-dweller.

Gnomes gnash gnats, in pointed hats . . .

From an unpublished poem
– Phil Roxbee Cox (1961–)

Goblins

Goblins are said to be even more ugly than gnomes (by human standards) and usually live in caves or among the roots of ancient trees, actively seeking out humans to lead astray. The first reports (or stories) involving goblins came from France but, over the years, the little creatures appear to have spread all over Europe. They always seem to be on the move, which is why they don't dig or build permanent homes but prefer to sleep in caves, among roots, or even in people's houses. They're tricksters and enjoy making life difficult for us human beings, and are said to be responsible for many of the strange noises heard down mines (though that could, of course, be the gnomes).

Favourite goblin tricks include turning signposts to point in the wrong direction and hiding everyday objects! No wonder I keep mislaying my keys . . .

An' the Gobble-uns 'll git you
Ef you don't watch out!

From 'Little Orphant Annie'
– J. W. Riley (1849–1916)

Elves

In England, the term elf used to be used to describe pretty much all the different types of fairy. Over time though, the word fairy replaced this, and an elf came to describe a more specific type of magical being. It seems that, in medieval England, elves got blamed for all sorts of different things, from horses manes becoming tangled to causing nightmares (see page 70).

There were a whole variety of different ailments attributed to elves, such as elf sickness, water-elf sickness and, worst of all, elf shot. Both animals and humans could be afflicted by elf shot, so named because it was believed to have been caused by elves shooting tiny darts at their victims.

Evidence?

So-called evidence of elves at work was the small flint 'elf arrows' that were sometimes unearthed. In truth, these were actually prehistoric arrowheads, the wooden shafts having long since rotted away.

Light & dark elves

In Scandinavia, there were the light elves who lived above the ground and the dark elves who lived below it, only coming to the surface at night. Scandinavian elves were generally human-sized. The only way you could tell them apart from us was, apparently, by their tails.

A polite act

A popular story involves a local dance where a man was partnering a beautiful woman. He only realized that she was, in fact, an elf when he saw the tip of her tail sticking out beneath the hem of her dress. Instead of being alarmed, or exposing her as not being human, he politely told her that her garter was slipping and pointed to her tail.

Tucking it away, she then carried on dancing and whispered an elfin blessing into the man's ear. He had good luck and good fortune for the rest of his days.

Nightmares

Why do nightmares – horrific dreams which often leave us sweating and exhausted – earn a place in a book about fairies? The clue is in the name: mares as in horses. It used to be believed that, at night, an elf would climb on to someone's bed and ride them like a horse, leaving the victim hot and sweaty like a horse after a long gallop. Anyone used so unfairly by an elf in this way would have unpleasant, restless dreams to go with it.

The Fairy Blast & Stroke

Accerding to Celtic myth, if a fairy hits you, a small lump, or tumour, will appear on your body. What with fairies usually being invisible, unless you have the Sight (see pages 24 to 25), the first thing you know about having been hit is when you see the lump itself. This is called the fairy blast.

The fairy stroke is worse still: it's when the victim is paralysed. Often, the only treatment available is from the fairy doctor (see pages 55 to 57), and that certainly isn't guaranteed to cure you.

The Tooth Fairy

If you put one of your milk teeth under your pillow when it comes out, the tooth fairy replaces it with a coin. This used to be a silver threepenny bit (3d) but, when these were phased out, the fairies left a silver sixpence. When decimalization came in (in 1971) and sixpences went the way of silver and brass threepenny bits, the fairy started leaving a fifty-pence piece and, more recently, sometimes even a pound coin. This used to be the job of a number of fairies. Now, it seems, the tooth fairy works alone.

Fairy Money

Money found on the ground was often said to have been left there by a good fairy. A good fairy or not, it's always wise to spend such money quickly because, once picked up, it soon becomes worthless, turning to leaves. By the same token, if you're a poor peasant who finds money dropped by a rich man, you'd be wise to spend it quickly, rather than risk being found with what is obviously not rightfully yours!

The Cottingley Fairies

Probably the most famous of fairy hoax of all time was the photographs of 'fairies' taken by two girls, sixteen-year-old Elsie Wright and her ten-year-old cousin, Frances Griffiths, in 1917.

The girls lived together in Cottingley, just outside Bradford in West Yorkshire, and often played in a brook near their house, where they claimed to see fairies. To 'prove' it, Elsie borrowed her father's camera . . . and he was in for a shock when he next developed his pictures. (Back then, cameras were

74

far more basic, and photographs were black and white, of course.) There was a picture of Frances with a troop of fairies dancing in front of her! A month later, Frances took a photo of Elsie playing with a gnome!

A flurry of interest

No one thought much more about the photos until, a few years later, Elsie's mother became interested in the supernatural and took the pictures to a meeting of theosophists (who believed in such things), where they caused much excitement.

The negatives of the two photographs were checked by an expert in photography, who confirmed that they'd not been altered in any way. In other words, the fairies really were in the pictures with the girls, and hadn't been added afterwards. This opinion was also later confirmed by the Kodak film company, though they couldn't confirm whether or not the fairies were real!

Elsie's picture of Frances and the fairies

Enter Sherlock Holmes

Sir Arthur Conan Doyle, author of the Sherlock Holmes stories, was a great believer in the supernatural and took these photographs to be proof of the existence of fairies. In 1920, they appeared in *Strand* magazine, along with an article he'd written about them. He also arranged for the girls to be given a camera in the hope that they could capture more fairies on film. Which they did, with three more pictures, bringing the total to five.

In 1922, Conan Doyle published a book entitled *The Coming of the Fairies*, which many people thought was completely and utterly ridiculous. It's important to remember, though, that this was soon after the Great War (1914–18) in which millions had died, and was a time when people were looking for proof of life after death and of magical 'other worlds'.

The truth at last?

If you look at the photos today, it's amazing to think that the hoax wasn't obvious to everyone. In 1983, aged 83, Elsie admitted that the negatives didn't need to be tampered with because the fairies were indeed in the photographs when they were taken. This is because they were nothing more than pictures cut out of magazines, kept in place with hatpins. What had started out as a bit of harmless fun for Elsie and Frances had been taken so seriously by such important people that they felt afraid to admit it was all a joke!

A different claim

Frances Griffiths had a slightly different version of events. Although she finally admitted, as an adult, that the first four photos were faked, to her dying day she insisted that they really had both played with fairies, and that the fifth and final photo had been absolutely genuine.

The Flower Fairies

Cicely Mary Barker's Flower Fairies are now some of the most famous and instantly recognizable fairies in the world. She never claimed that they were real, and used children to model for them.

Born in Croydon, in Surrey, in 1895, Cicely was a poorly child and was educated at home rather than school. In 1908, she joined the Croydon Art Society, which exhibited some of her early work. In 1911 (when she was fifteen), four of her pictures were printed on greetings cards by Raphael Tuck, a publisher. After that, Cicely had pictures regularly appearing in books and magazines and on cards. (The then Queen Mother was a huge fan of fairy postcards and sent many to her friends.)

Helping the family finances

Tragically, Cicely's father died when she was seventeen. She sent Flower Fairy paintings to a whole variety of publishers and they were – finally – bought by Blackie in 1923. The first, in what was to become a series of eight Flower Fairy books, was entitled *Flower Fairies of the Spring* and contained twenty-four pictures and accompanying verses. For this, Cicely Mary Barker was paid just twenty-five pounds.

The children behind the paintings

There was no shortage of children for Cicely to use as artist's models. Following their father's death, Cecily's sister Dorothy set up a kindergarten, and

80

many of those attending ended up as Flower Fairies. She also used relatives and the children of friends.

Cicely went to great lengths to match the children to the flowers, and to try to capture their personality. She was also careful to make the flowers themselves as accurate as possible. She sometimes called on experts at Kew Gardens to provide the more exotic or unusual specimens.

Cicely Mary Barker died in 1973, but her Flower Fairies are now more popular then ever.

Spenser's The Faerie Queene

The *Faerie Queene* was a poem in six books written by Edmund Spenser (1552–99), using a stanza of eight lines of ten syllables followed by a ninth line of twelve, invented by Spenser himself. The first three books were published in 1590 and the remaining three in 1596.

The premise of the story is that the Faerie Queene has twelve knights undertake twelve quests in the twelve days of her annual festival; each knight represents a different virtue (such as friend-ship or justice).

The Faerie Queene in the poem isn't so much a fairy, however, as a representation of the concept of 'glory' in general and his beloved monarch Queen Elizabeth I of England – often referred to as Gloriana – in particular. Spenser says as much in his introductory letter addressed to Sir Walter Raleigh.

Having said that, *The Faerie Queene* is one of the most famous pieces of writing with the word 'fairy' in the title – however oddly spelled – so *The Truth About Fairies* wouldn't be complete without mentioning it!

The Christmas Tree Fairy

Pagan and Christian festivals and rituals are often blurred. Christmas Day itself, for example, is on 25 December, which was the Roman festival of *Dies Natalis Solis Invicti*.

Of course, by rights, it should be an angel, and not a fairy, on top of the Christmas tree, but stories of tree nymphs predate Christianity by a long time. Then there's the matter of fairy lights. As I said in *The Truth About Christmas*, surely these too should be *angel* lights?

The Sugar Plum Fairy

A sugar plum is not a crystallized fruit but a good old-fashioned boiled sweet. 'The Dance of the Sugar Plum Fairy' is the third (and by far the most popular) movement in Tchaikovsky's ballet *The Nutcracker*, set at Christmas time. The original orchestration features a celesta, which is a small keyboard instrument that gives an other-worldly bell-like sound (ideal for fairies). Nowadays a piano is often used instead. The music is one of the most popular classical music ringtone downloads!

Tinkerbell

By far the most famous stage fairy of all time is Tinkerbell in the children's play *Peter Pan* by J. M. Barrie (1860–1937), which later became a book, and has been the inspiration for a number of films. Good at heart, Tinkerbell clearly loves Peter, the boy who never wants to grow up, and is jealous when he becomes friendly with Wendy. In the end, though, Tinkerbell saves Wendy's life. She's so small that she's usually played by a tiny light . . . that begins to fade unless the audience claps to show that it believes in fairies.